We Are a Class

ROB SANDERS

ILLUSTRATED BY HANNAH ABBO

beaming books

MINNEAPOLIS

IN CELEBRATION OF TEACHERS AND LIBRARIANS WHO CREATE SAFE
AND ACCEPTING HOMES FOR LEARNERS —RS

FOR ALL THE TEACHERS THAT MAKE THE WORLD A BETTER,
GENTLER PLACE —HA

Text copyright © 2024 Rob Sanders
Illustrations copyright © 2024 Hannah Abbo

Published in 2024 by Beaming Books, an imprint of 1517 Media. All rights reserved.
No part of this book may be reproduced without the written permission of the publisher.
Email copyright@1517.media.

30 29 28 27 26 25 24   1 2 3 4 5 6 7 8 9

Hardcover ISBN: 978-1-5064-8921-6
eBook ISBN: 978-1-5064-8922-3

Library of Congress Cataloging-in-Publication Data

Names: Sanders, Rob, 1958- author. | Abbo, Hannah, illustrator.
Title: We are a class / Rob Sanders ; illustrated by Hannah Abbo.
Description: Minneapolis : Beaming Books, 2024. | Audience: Ages 3-8 |
  Summary: Celebrates the different identities, personalities, talents,
  and gifts that make up a class of students.
Identifiers: LCCN 2023046911 (print) | LCCN 2023046912 (ebook) | ISBN
  9781506489216 (hardback) | ISBN 9781506489223 (ebook)
Subjects: CYAC: Stories in rhyme. | Individual differences--Fiction. |
  Schools--Fiction. | LCGFT: Stories in rhyme. | Picture books.
Classification: LCC PZ8.3.S We 2024 (print) | LCC PZ8.3.S (ebook) | DDC
  [E]--dc23
LC record available at https://lccn.loc.gov/2023046911
LC ebook record available at https://lccn.loc.gov/2023046912

Beaming Books
PO Box 1209
Minneapolis, MN 55440-1209
Beamingbooks.com

Printed in China.

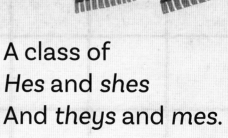

We are a class.

A class of
Hes and *shes*
And *theys* and *mes*.

With a teacher who's
Mrs. or Mr. or Miss.

Or a teacher who's
Dr. or Ms. or Mx.

A teacher loaded with teaching tricks!

We're creative thinkers
With brains to the brim.
Brave enough to go out on a limb.

We're movers and shakers.
Mammoth change makers.
Friends. Learners.
Achievement earners.

Comrades. A team.
Ready to dream!

We arrive here
As hikers and bikers.
Gliders and riders.
Racers and chasers.
Challenge facers.

We come to this place
With its desks and bookcase.
We feel safe in this space,
Like a warm embrace.

We come here to share.
To care.
To always play fair.
To be open. Aware.
To take learning dares.

We lend an ear.
Have hearts that hear.
We listen to the spoken.
The unspoken.
The broken.

We are a class.

We're tomorrow's leaders.
Today's leaders too.
We're readers.
Cheerleaders.
Seekers
And speakers.

Scientists.
Artists.
Athletes.
Mathletes.
Singers.
Dreamers.

We are a class.

Questioning.
Stating.
Discussing.
Debating.

We read about history.
We write our own history.

We are a class.

We're peeps and pals.
We can and we shall
Link arms together
Through all kinds of weather.

We're helpful.
Thoughtful.
Thankful.

We're mindful.
Respectful.
Resourceful.

United.
Excited.
Delighted.
Ignited.

And sometimes ...
We're more than a class.

We're family.

When all of us gather,
We're stronger together.

We are a class.

I come!

And you?
Yes, YOU!
There's no need to fear.
We're glad you are here.

You're part of what's us.
No need to discuss.
We're better with you.

Do you feel it too?
It's perfectly clear.
Now join us to cheer:

ROB SANDERS is a teacher who writes and a writer who teaches. He is known for his funny and fierce fiction and nonfiction picture books and is recognized as one of the pioneers in the arena of LGBTQ+ literary nonfiction picture books. He is the author of dozens of picture books, including *Pride: The Story of Harvey Milk and the Rainbow Flag*, *Peaceful Fights for Equal Rights*, and *Stonewall: a Building, an Uprising, a Revolution*. *Blood Brothers*, his first middle grade novel, was selected as a 2023 NCTE Notable Novel in Verse. A native of Springfield, Missouri, Rob has lived and worked in Texas, Alabama, and Tennessee. He now lives in Florida and writes books full time.

HANNAH ABBO is an illustrator from the United Kingdom, currently living and working in Lisbon, Portugal. She lives with her partner and child, and their cat. When she's not drawing she loves making ceramics in a local studio, visiting the botanical gardens, and baking bread.